WHAT IS CYBERSECURITY?

HAQ KAMAR

Britannica®
Educational Publishing

IN ASSOCIATION WITH

ROSEN
EDUCATIONAL SERVICES

Published in 2018 by Britannica Educational Publishing (a trademark of Encyclopædia Britannica, Inc.) in association with The Rosen Publishing Group, Inc.
29 East 21st Street, New York, NY 10010

Distributed exclusively by Rosen Publishing.
To see additional Britannica Educational Publishing titles, go to rosenpublishing.com.

First Edition

Britannica Educational Publishing
J.E. Luebering: Executive Director, Core Editorial
Mary Rose McCudden: Editor, Britannica Student Encyclopedia

Rosen Publishing
Bernadette Davis: Editor
Nelson Sá: Art Director
Nicole Russo-Duca: Series Designer
Cindy Reiman: Photography Manager
Sherri Jackson: Photo Researcher

Library of Congress Cataloging-in-Publication Data

Names: Kamar, Haq, author.
Title: What is cybersecurity? / Haq Kamar.
Description: New York : Britannica Educational Publishing, in Association with Rosen Educational Services, 2018. | Series: Let's find out! Computer science | Includes bibliographical references and index. | Audience: Grades 1–4.
Identifiers: LCCN 2017018663| ISBN 9781680488548 (library bound : alk. paper)
| ISBN 9781680488531 (pbk. : alk. paper) | ISBN 9781538300367 (6 pack : alk. paper)
Subjects: LCSH: Computer security—Juvenile literature. | Computer crimes—Juvenile literature.
Classification: LCC QA76.9.A25 K335 2017 | DDC 005.8—dc23
LC record available at https://lccn.loc.gov/2017018663

Manufactured in the United States of America

Photo credits: Cover and back cover deepadesigns/Shutterstock.com; p. 4 Redpixel.PL/Shutterstock.com; p. 5 zippy/Shutterstock.com; p. 6 Shaifulzamri/Shutterstock.com; p. 7 Highwaystarz-Photography/iStock/Thinkstock; p. 8 Arka38/Shutterstock.com; p. 9 Roman Kosolapov/Shutterstock.com; p. 10 © iStockphoto.com/Jimkruger; p. 11 Image Source Pink/Image Source/Thinkstock; p. 12 Brilt/Alamy Stock Photo; p. 13 Jose Luis Pelaez Inc./Blend Images/Thinkstock; pp. 14, 17, 26 Rawpixel.com/Shutterstock.com; p. 15 Ymgerman/Shutterstock.com; p. 16 Smith Collection/Gado/Archive Photos/Getty Images; p. 18 Njgphoto/E+/Getty Images; p. 19 KenTannenbaum/iStock/Thinkstock; p. 20 Chris Willson/Alamy Stock Photo; p. 21 © iStockphoto.com/Coast-to-Coast; p. 22 Barton Gellman/Getty Images; p. 23 Portland Press Herald/Getty Images; p. 24 DragonImages/iStock/Thinkstock; p. 25 Nipastock/Shutterstock.com; p. 27 © iStockphoto.com/Matejmo; p. 28 Jeff Greenberg/Universal Images Group/Getty Images; p. 29 Brendan Hoffman/Getty Images; interior pages background © iStockphoto.com/D3Damon.

CONTENTS

What Are Computers and Computer Networks?

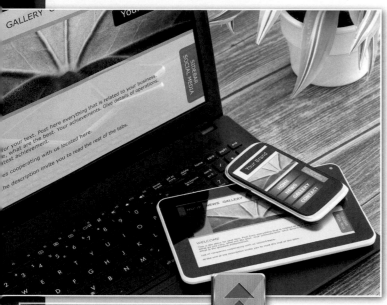

A computer stores, displays, and processes information. Computers come in many forms. We use desktops, laptops, tablets, or smartphones at home, at school, and at work. Computers help with manufacturing products, keeping records, communicating, and banking. Computers can be fun, too. We use computers to shop, to listen to music, and to play games.

A computer network is a collection of computers that are connected to each other. They

All of these devices are computers. They are each used for different reasons, and some are more mobile than others.

The computers in this computer lab have access to the internet and to a local area network.

communicate with each other electronically. The internet is one example of a network. Communicating between computers through the internet happens in ways that the user usually controls. However, using the internet is not always safe. It is important to know how to make computers safer.

THINK ABOUT IT

Think about what would happen if you and your family went through a day without using a computer at all. What would you do? What activities would you have to do differently?

Physical Harm

Computers can be damaged in many different ways. A person can pour water on a device, hit it with a hard object, or drop it.

Computers can also be stolen. A smartphone can be taken from out of a person's pocket or a laptop may be swiped from an unattended chair in a restaurant. There are many other ways a computer may be stolen. Laws clearly explain punishments for people who steal or deliberately damage physical property such as computers. However, people can also damage computers through software. A hacker, or a person

A Kensington lock will keep a device secure while left in an open area if it is locked to furniture.

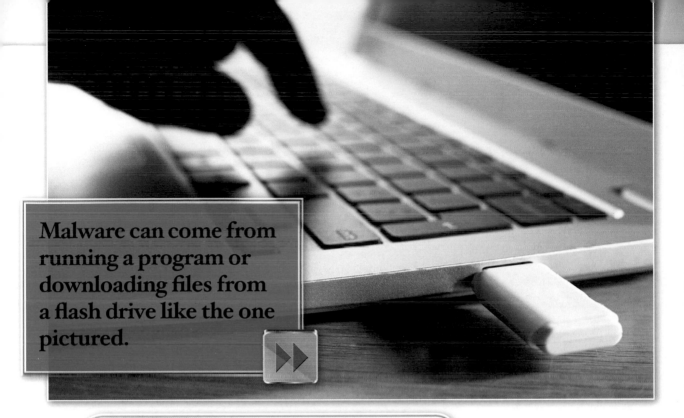

Malware can come from running a program or downloading files from a flash drive like the one pictured.

▶▶

THINK ABOUT IT

How do you and your family protect your electronic devices?

who breaks into computer systems, can download and install destructive software on a user's computer without taking the computer. They can also download files in this kind of attack. Hackers can also delete some or all of the computer owner's files.

WHAT IS CYBERSECURITY?

The word "cyber" means "related to computers or computer networks." Cybersecurity therefore is protection for your computer and the information on the computer. Without cybersecurity, data on a computer can be erased or stolen.

Keeping yourself safe online is a lot like keeping yourself safe offline. It is important to be aware of your surroundings at all times. Understand where threats may

A firewall can protect computers by filtering traffic between devices and the internet.

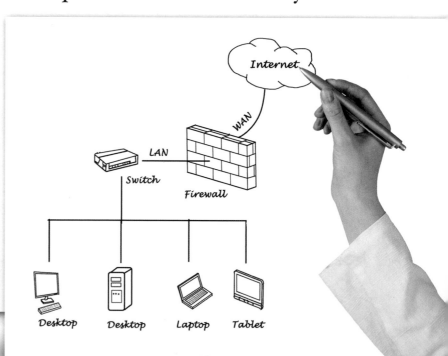

Someone has left a computer and a cell phone unattended. The devices and the data they store are at risk.

come from and know how to get help. However, it is a little harder to keep your virtual existence safe. Your virtual existence is the information that computers and databases associate with you. Threats in the virtual world are not always as easy to recognize as threats in the real world. That is why cybersecurity is so important.

COMPARE AND CONTRAST

How were you taught to keep safe outside? What kinds of steps would you take or do you take to be safe online?

WHY ATTACK A COMPUTER?

Cybersecurity can often stop hackers from committing a cybercrime. However, some hackers are familiar with certain cybersecurity measures and know how to get around them.

Hackers may break into computers for a number of reasons. They may want to sell the data they access or use the victim's computer to spread harmful programs. They may also want to harm or embarrass an organization they do not like. Or,

Many cyberattacks have targeted large stores to get at the data of the stores' customers.

COMPARE AND CONTRAST

How is stealing computer information like stealing the actual computer? How is it different?

they may want to become famous because of their abilities. A hacker might also just disagree with the beliefs of the victim. Some companies employ their own hackers so they can find the weak points in their security system. This makes their system stronger.
One common cybercrime involves tricking the victim.

Children are at risk because they are very trusting.

PHISHING

In a scam called **phishing**, someone sends emails pretending to be from a trustworthy organization. These emails ask for personal or financial information from an unsuspecting user. The user is tricked into sending that information.

Harmful emails offer opportunities and money. They are trying to trick the reader into sharing personal information.

Sharing credit card information online can be dangerous. There's always a chance for shared information to be abused.

Phishing emails can also supply a link to a fake website that looks like one the user might be familiar with, like a social network. The user is then asked to sign in to the account. That requires sharing a username, password, or some other sensitive information.

Advertisement links on some websites can also be phishing scams. These ads might claim you have won a prize. Trying to claim the prize will require you to enter your personal information. But they will never deliver the prize they promise because it is a trick.

MALWARE

Malicious software, or malware, is more invasive than phishing. It enters a computer through network connections, other software, and hardware. Downloading email attachments, visiting websites, or attaching a hardware device can put malware on a computer.

There are many types of malware. One type is spyware. Spyware gathers information by watching what a user does. Spyware can steal webcam footage and allow a hacker to watch the user. It can also record input. Worms and viruses are other types of malware. When

This woman is talking on Skype. Webcams can be hacked to record videos or take pictures.

Stores like Google Play and iTunes offer free and paid app downloads. But some apps steal users' information.

downloaded, they attempt to spread themselves either throughout the same infected computer or to a network. Spreading can corrupt data.

Trojans, or Trojan horse viruses, are

THINK ABOUT IT

During the Trojan War, the ancient Greeks built a hollow wooden horse that allowed them to enter the city of Troy and capture it. Why do you think Trojan malware has that name?

malware, too. Trojans are packaged with software that the user did intend to install. It is like opening a box of cereal and finding a prize you did not expect, but the prize is actually something harmful or unpleasant.

What Does Malware Do?

One effect of malware is that it slows down the infected computer when it runs. The infected computer may also become a zombie computer, or a computer that hackers control. Many zombie computers can attack a website by overloading it with traffic. One way to understand this is to think of a small restaurant where hundreds of people want to eat. There would not be enough space for all of them to eat. A restaurant employee would have to

This tweet reveals that a website is not available. A reply mentions that the site is under attack.

make some of them wait to enter, but a website cannot make people wait. Instead, the website would stop working for *everyone* who tries to use it.

Other zombie computers spread malware, videos, or pictures. Some content is illegal to send, so a zombie computer can cause legal trouble for the owner of the computer. The hacker controlling the computer would be hard to find, so they might not get into trouble.

COMPARE AND CONTRAST

How are phishing scams the same or different from malware?

Malware and Individuals

Malware that deletes data can cause many problems. Victims may only lose a few hours of homework, or they may lose years of photos and videos. It can cost money, too, if the malware damages a computer so that it needs to be fixed or replaced.

A serious cybercrime committed against individuals is identity theft. Hackers can use

This woman is destroying data to protect information. Destroying data can also be harmful.

Identity thieves will target sensitive information like a Social Security number or a credit card to steal money.

malware to steal a person's **identity**. They can access a person's important information, such as Social Security numbers and bank accounts. The criminal can then pretend to be that person and spend all the victim's money. It is possible to undo the damage that occurs because of identity theft, but it takes a lot of time.

Another consequence of a cyberattack is that it can hurt someone's reputation and relationships. For example, a user may pass along the malware without knowing it. The person who receives that may be upset with the user.

MALWARE AND COMPANIES

Companies sometimes use software that acts as malware. For example, a music company called Sony BMG once installed software on their music CDs that was meant to stop the user from copying the music. However, it also had other effects. Hackers were able to use the same software to cause trouble on other computers.

Companies can also be victims. Some hackers target companies to steal customers' personal information. Other hackers are more

In 2005 some CDs from Sony BMG (now Sony Music Entertainment) contained software that acted as malware.

THINK ABOUT IT

Should a company ever be able to access the data on a user's computer if the company isn't helping to fix a software problem? Why or why not?

interested in shutting down the whole business. They may perform something called a denial of service attack. These attacks overload a company's website so users cannot access the site.

The government can also encourage hacking. The Federal Bureau of Investigation (FBI) once asked a company for a way to get past the security on a phone that the company made. The FBI wanted to access a criminal's data in order to see if that person had planned a second crime.

This is the Federal Bureau of Investigation (FBI) headquarters building in Washington, DC. They investigate some cybercrimes.

Cybersecurity and Governments

Governments face threats to cybersecurity in many ways. Government computers can be affected by malware just as the computers of individuals are. That malware can be used to steal information about a country's secrets or about the people who work for the country.

Computer attacks can come from inside or outside of the country. Someone who works for a government may have access to secret computer files. They may copy that information and

This 2013 portrait shows Edward Snowden. He was not a hacker, but he did take files that were not his.

share it with others. They may have many reasons for doing that. They may want to sell the information or they may want to let other people know about activities that they do not approve of.

Governments themselves may use malware to hack into the computers of other governments or of companies. A man named Edward Snowden released files showing that the US government was secretly collecting data about many citizens and foreigners.

COMPARE AND CONTRAST

How is stealing a government's computer information similar to stealing information from an individual or a company? How is it different?

Sensitive government documents are frequently blacked out for security reasons.

Good Practices

Users can protect their devices by installing anti-malware software. This software scans a computer for malware and attempts to remove it. Users can also add a **firewall** to protect their information.

It is also a good idea to back up data often. This involves creating copies of the

> **VOCABULARY**
>
> A **firewall** is a program that restricts access to a computer.

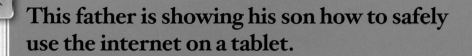

This father is showing his son how to safely use the internet on a tablet.

This external hard drive is hooked up to a laptop. Users can back up data on external hard drives.

data and saving them somewhere safe. Data can be backed up to a separate folder on the same computer, to an online site, or to an external storage device. External devices include external hard drives, flash drives, or SD cards.

When online, be careful where you click. Do not open unexpected attachments or click unfamiliar links. Do not download files from strange websites, and make sure the URL matches the site you are trying to visit.

Speak with your family about making sure your computer has all of these protections. These basic steps will keep a device safe.

Data Encryption

Encryption is an advanced form of protection. Computers encrypt data by turning it into a code that must be solved, or decrypted, to be read.

Encryption has been done by hand since ancient times. Encryption is useful because it is not easy to read or determine the value of encrypted data. In addition to encrypting files, a user can encrypt access points. Doing that means a hacker cannot even get to the files on a computer. Layers of encryption mean layers of cybersecurity.

Website accounts rely on encryption to protect users' data.

THINK ABOUT IT

Speaking another language is like encryption.
What else is like encryption?

There are two ways to decrypt data. Either someone shares the instructions on how to decrypt the data, or someone figures it out by hacking. However, hacking is difficult and takes much more time and effort than being given the answer.

Encryption scrambles information. It makes the data look something like this.

LAW ENFORCEMENT

There are some laws against online misconduct but not for every type of attack. As a result, some victims of online attacks cannot receive justice or compensation for their trouble.

Companies and providers of internet service work to end abuse. They may recognize and address some abuses, but there are too many abuses to keep up with.

Using the internet

This police officer is looking at email. She may be investigating a cybercrime.

In 2013, Major General Brett Williams spoke to a crowd about cybersecurity.

creates an environment that exposes people to millions of strangers. Certain websites have more visitors than the population of the biggest cities in the world. Online hackers can do much more than thieves stealing in the real world.

It is possible to keep hackers out of your computer, however. You must protect hardware *and* data from theft. Have a plan and know what to do if protection fails. Parents can help with prevention, and computer experts can solve any problems that occur.

THINK ABOUT IT

Computers can be difficult to keep safe, but people still like to use them. Why do you think that is?

GLOSSARY

communicate To send and receive information.

cyberattack An online attack.

decrypt To crack a code so that the message can be read.

denial of service attack An attack that overloads a website so that no one can use it.

hacker An expert at programming and solving problems with a computer; a person who gains access to a computer system through an unusual entry point.

infected Contaminated with a harmful computer program.

input To enter data into a computer.

internet A communications system that connects computers and computer networks all over the world.

malicious Mean or spiteful; deliberately harmful.

scam A plan to deceive or trick someone.

spyware Software that collects and shares information about a computer's activities without the user's permission.

URL An address on the internet. It is short for Uniform Resource Locator and is formatted as "http://www. website.com."

virtual Of or existing mostly online.

virus A program that produces copies of itself in a computer.

worm A program that infects and damages networks.

FOR MORE INFORMATION

Books

Brundle, Harriet. *Staying Safe Online*. Kings Lynn, UK: BookLife, 2016.

Goldstein, Margaret J., and Martin Gitlin. *Cyber Attack*. Minneapolis, MN: Twenty-First Century Books, 2015.

Head, Honor. *Being Safe Online*. London, UK: Franklin Watts, 2015.

McAneney, Caitie. *Online Safety* (Let's Talk About It). New York, NY: Powerkids Press, 2015.

Stuckey, Rachel. *Cyber Bullying*. New York, NY: Crabtree Publishing Company, 2013.

Websites

Because of the changing nature of internet links, Rosen Publishing has developed an online list of websites related to the subject of this book. This site is updated regularly. Please use this link to access this list:

http://www.rosenlinks.com/LFO/Cyber

Index